WHY DO ESKIMOS RUB NOSES?

WHY DO ESKIMOS RUB NOSES?

And Other Mind-Boggling Questions About Human Behaviour

Ralph Levinson

Illustrated by Mike Roberts

BEAVER BOOKS

A Beaver Book

Published by Arrow Books Limited
62–5 Chandos Place, London WC2N 4NW

An imprint of Century Hutchinson Ltd

London Melbourne Sydney Auckland
Johannesburg and agencies throughout the world

First published 1989
Text © Ralph Levinson 1989
Illustrations © Century Hutchinson 1989

Set in Century Schoolbook
by JH Graphics Ltd, Reading

Made and printed in Great Britain
by Anchor Press Limited
Tiptree, Essex

ISBN 0 09 959650 4

Contents

Introduction

This is a book about behaviour. Not good or bad behaviour, but the little actions we perform in everyday life. There are some really amazing explanations. You'll find out why it's rude to stick out our tongues and why we have butterflies in our stomachs. You'll learn why laughing and crying are so near and yet so far. You'll not only discover new and exciting things about yourself but enjoy lots of fun activities too.

Those who watch and study people's actions are called human behaviourists. They are interested in the way we walk, fold our hands, greet each other, sit down to eat and in everything we do. They have discovered many fascinating facts about us humans and you'll find them in these pages.

You can become a behaviourist, too. All you need is a pencil, a notebook and a lot of patience. You will learn many surprising bits of information by carrying out some of the 'human' experiments in this book. You must remember studying people too closely can seem rude but even so there are plenty of activities you can follow without annoying anyone.

This book will make your hair stand on end. Turn to page 66 to see why. Start reading this end and you'll come out a 'human' scientist at the other end!

9

Hello!

*This section looks at what's behind
our behaviour when we meet and when we
become attracted to each other.*

Why do Eskimos rub noses?

We wear gloves in cold weather, but it is still thought polite to remove them when we shake hands. For people, like the Eskimos, who live in the polar north in conditions of extreme cold, it would be hazardous to remove their hand-coverings each time they greeted each other. It is thought that Eskimos have always used another part of their body for greeting, one that is not tightly muffled even in the vast, snow-covered Arctic areas. Everyone has to breathe, and the best place to breathe is through your nose.

And that's why rubbing noses is such an appropriate way of saying 'Hello'. It's the only part of the body that's not beneath layers of clothing!

Why do we shake hands?

Shaking hands has been a common greeting in many parts of the world for centuries. One explanation is that when two strangers wished to meet peacefully they would open their hands to show that they were not hiding any weapons. Once the hands were free they could grasp them as an act of friendship.

The way we shake hands depends on the occasion. We also do it when we say goodbye. Meeting strangers, we grip their hands and then let go. With old friends we may continue to grasp their hands and even combine it with a hug. Lovers shake hands in other ways, perhaps running their fingers across the palms of their hands. You wouldn't shake a stranger's hand in that way!

Hands are very useful instruments for greeting. They are sensitive. You can judge people by how firm their handshake is, and you can give messages yourself. For example, you wouldn't shake the hand of a small child in the same way you shake that of a Sumo wrestler. The way you shake hands can influence what someone else thinks of you. A handshake might even change the course of your life!

Why do lovers gaze into each other's eyes?

Our eyes are one of the most expressive features of our face; we often refer to laughing eyes, sad eyes, cruel eyes, curious eyes. For lovers, the most important part of the eye appears to be the little black spot in the centre called the pupil.

The pupil controls the amount of light entering the eye. When there is very little light, the pupil dilates to allow in as much light as possible. When the light is very bright, the pupil contracts since intense light can damage the eye. You can try this out for yourself. Look at your pupils in a mirror when a room is very poorly lit, then see what happens when the lighting is turned up.

The pupil also changes size according to the way we feel. If we enjoy looking at something like a delicious pudding or a favourite pet, then our pupils dilate as if we want to allow in as much light as possible. When we look at something boring, our pupils contract.

The pupil size of other people's eyes also influences the size of our own pupils. Experiments have shown that when we look at different pictures of the same person we tend to prefer those where the eyes have bigger pupils. Our own pupils respond by opening wider.

The seductive effect of the dilated pupil has been known about for hundreds of years. In Renaissance Italy, women of the court used an eyedrop potion called 'Belladonna' which they dabbed into their eyes. Belladonna was made from a plant called deadly nightshade, and it made the ladies' pupils dilate to increase their attractiveness. 'Belladonna' means 'beautiful woman'.

When lovers gaze into each other's eyes they are unconsciously checking pupil size. If they really are fond of each other, then their pupils will dilate. As one sees the other's pupils dilate, his or hers will respond, until both sets of pupils reach the maximum size. If pupils remain small then that is a big turn-off and they will soon stop gazing at each other. A lover's gaze really is a love check-up – the longer the gaze the greater the love.

Next time someone says they like you, take a quick peek at their eyes.

Why do we kiss?

Kissing is one of the most pleasant human activities. Kissing is also something that is done by the vast majority of adults throughout the world.

Before humans learned to control fire, they had to soften food before passing it on to babies and small children. Even when babies have teethed, their teeth and jaws are still fairly weak. Mothers used to chew food and soften it with saliva before passing it on to their children. Some animals, like dingoes, feed their young in a similar way.

Feeding children in this way was rather like doing the cooking, except the saliva and the chewing took the place of fire and preparation. It must have been time-consuming to chew the food finely enough to be passed into a baby's mouth.

Human beings probably practised this form of feeding for hundreds of thousands of years, and they may have continued for many years after they had learned to use fire. Once this mouth-to-mouth contact was no longer necessary for feeding it could have persisted as kissing. Since it was such a loving action it made sense to keep it, so feeding turned into kissing!

16

All About Feelings

*This section looks at how we show
our feelings.*

Why do we cry?

Since crying is about the first thing we do when we arrive in this funny old world it must be a very important part of our behaviour. Parents, midwives and doctors would be worried if we didn't cry because it allows us to open up our lungs so proper breathing can start.

Once our breathing in the first few seconds of our lives is sorted out, why do we continue to cry? We do so a lot during our time as a baby, a little as small children, every now and again as adults, and, perhaps, a little more as elderly people. Crying has a lot to do with our ability to fend for ourselves. Babies aren't very good at getting up in the morning, making their breakfasts and going out for an early morning jog. Instead, babies need to send out a message if they feel miserable and unhappy. Since they can't talk, crying is a very good way to communicate. And there are not many people who can ignore a crying baby.

Babies cry when they are hungry, when they need changing, when they hurt themselves, and sometimes when they are surrounded by strangers or find themselves in unfamiliar places. If they are outside their usual play and eating areas, babies often feel unhappy because everything is alien. We might feel the same if we suddenly came across a creature from outer space. Our first reaction would be fright – we would want to protect ourselves, and suspect the creature is an enemy even though it may turn out to be friendly. A baby responds like this towards new objects and people. This is why soothing a baby is so important – it helps it recover from pain and have more confidence.

Crying is one of the main distress responses we have in common with other mammals. Animals ranging through gorillas, cats, elephants and whales all 'cry' when they are in distress. The noises may be different but humans can recognize a crying mammal. There have even been cases of monkeys and dolphins responding to the crying of human children and gathering around to help.

Crying exists throughout the animal world and extends into adulthood. Even in older people it is a signal of pain and distress. Crying is a call for help to which we feel the need to respond.

Things to do and think about

1 Here's a way to laze about and enjoy observing a bit of social behaviour. Spend some time watching films or dramas on TV. Make a note of the situations where people cry.

2 Women tend to cry a lot more than men. Some people like to say this proves women are weaker than men. This is completely untrue. A more convincing explanation is that women are less afraid to show how they feel. Do you ever see men crying? What makes them cry?

Why do we laugh?

'I laughed until I cried' is the expression people use when they laugh so much that it feels painful. When someone shakes with intense or hysterical laughter, it's almost impossible to tell whether they're laughing or crying. Imagine you're in a room with some posh people where everyone is very quiet then something happens which makes you and a friend giggle. Since it is very rude to giggle or make a noise you have to keep it to yourselves and this makes you giggle even more, especially when you see your friend shaking with laughter and their face going bright red. You feel your eyes watering up and the tears streaming down your cheeks. And it's painful too because you haven't been able to laugh out loud.

It must seem surprising that laughter is like crying. After all we normally cry when we are hurt and laugh at something funny. Hurting ourselves is not funny.

It is all to do with our early experiences as a baby. The first thing we do is to cry. Only after the first few months of our life do we laugh. When a baby recognizes its parent there is no need to cry and the baby is relieved. The parent plays with the baby and often startles it by tickling or patting. It is this mixture of relief at seeing the parent, and surprise at the movements and expressions the parent makes during play that brings on laughter.

Frequently the baby will laugh to encourage the parent or an older person to play with it. Think how you feel when a baby starts to burble and laugh. It's almost irresistible. You want to play and shake a rattle to keep it laughing. Sometimes the baby becomes alarmed by the activity and starts to cry. This brings on a protective response by the parent and the baby quietens down. The baby has laughed so much it has started to cry!

Things to do

1 We have seen that laughing is so close to crying that, sometimes, it is difficult to see the difference. Look very carefully at people when they give a real belly laugh.

What kinds of noises do they make?
How do their cheeks look?
How does their mouth move?
How does their nose move?
Are their eyes closed or open?
What is the position of their head?
How do their shoulders move?
What do they do with their feet?

2 What makes people laugh? Carry out your own survey. It is commonly thought that a funny joke makes people laugh. But look more closely. Make a list of all the occasions when someone gives a really good laugh. What brings it about?

3 Sometimes, someone gives a false laugh. That is, someone is trying to laugh but not succeeding. What are the differences between a false and a real laugh?

Why do we smile?

Smiling and laughing seem to go together. We think of them signifying happy moods, the smile being a polite version of a laugh. For both, we pull back our mouths: in laughing we shake about a lot, in smiling the ends of our mouths curve upwards.

Imagine you are going to meet someone for the first time. You both feel nervous as people always do when they meet for the first time. If he smiles then you feel immediately reassured. The smile is a way of saying 'This is a nervous moment for us but, don't worry, you need not fear me.'

The smile relays a different message from the laugh. We tend to pull our mouth back when we are afraid as we do in both the smile and the laugh. As we turn the lips upward, the fear message becomes one of reassurance, too. That is why we often smile when we greet each other, when we say thank you and when we apologize. There are lots of other occasions when we smile, but they all transmit the same message, 'It's all right. You can relax.'

Things to do

1 Does a smile help to make friends? For this exercise, you'll need to be an actor and a scientist. The actor in you will be putting on a smile even when you don't feel like it that much. The scientist will be observing and judging the reactions of others.

One day you act out your smiling mood. Whenever you meet someone, smile at them. Not a fixed smile or a grin but a pleasant smiling nod. At the end of the day note down the following points:

Do people return your smile?
Do you spend a longer time than usual with each person when you smile?
Does any particular age group respond much more positively to your smile?
Do you notice any differences in the ways your friends greet you?
You must try and smile pleasantly at people you don't like. Does smiling make any difference to the way you feel about them or the way you think they feel about you?

2 Spend the next day being unsmiling. It helps if you're actually in the mood, so try getting out of the wrong side of your bed. Compare the results with the points you made when you spent the day smiling.

Why do we blush?

Imagine you have a sister who has won lots of medals for swimming. One day you bring some friends back to your house when nobody else is in. They ask you about the medals and, since you want to make an impression, you say that you won them. The truth is that you can't swim but you enjoy the popularity that follows. A few weeks later the same friends come round to your house when your sister is there and they ask you if you'd like to come swimming with them. Of course you're terrified they will discover the truth. You can't go swimming because they'll surely find you out. One friend then mentions what a good swimmer you must be to your sister. You feel your skin go all prickly and hot as your friends look at you.

We've all gone through something like this. It may be someone praising us or calling out our name in assembly. You may be reading out a passage to a group of people and, suddenly, you lose your place. We all have the same reaction, there's a hot tingly sensation and a sinking feeling in the stomach. Everyone sees you blushing as your face turns the colour of tomato paste.

When you are put in this kind of threatening situation your nervous system responds to the fear. The heart starts beating faster, pumping blood through the organs of the body. The blood carries food and oxygen to the tissues of the body to provide extra energy as you steel yourself to face the threat. As your tissues start to work overtime, extra heat is produced and you need to cool off. A side effect is that the blood vessels, near the surface of the skin, widen so that heat can be removed. It is these blood vessels that give the effect of blushing.

Blushing is a pretty good way of reading people. You can tell what kind of things make them go all hot and flushed. It's impossible to disguise blushing, so it really can indicate what fears people have.

One of the main causes of blushing is 'being found out'. If someone has been caught lying then they are very likely to blush. This reaction was used in the old lie detector test. The victim would have electrodes attached to his skin and would be asked a number of questions. If he lied, he would blush and changes would take place in the surface of the skin. This information would be passed through the electrodes and record a peak on the lie detector monitor.

Things to do

1 Here's your chance to be a human lie detector. Ask your friends a number of questions: for example, about their school, their home, their family. In their answers they have to tell three lies.

26

Even when people know it's a game they feel a blush coming on when they tell an untruth. How good are you at 'finding out' your friends?

2 Look carefully at people's facial reactions over the next two weeks. Record the kinds of situations that make people blush.

Why do we roar with anger and groan with pain?

It seems that certain sounds or calls best express what we are feeling. It is particularly satisfying to give a really good yell when we're feeling angry. And it can help sometimes to groan when we're feeling pain.

Humans aren't the only animals that express their feelings in this way. The sounds we make are very similar to the sounds made by apes and monkeys when they feel angry, sad, hurt or tickled. And it is not only apes and monkeys – the whine of a beaten dog can tell us something about the way it is feeling. In the same way we can frighten our pets if they hear us cry or yell, whereas the sound of loud laughter may alarm them at first but not for long.

We could express what we feel without all the accompanying sound effects. If we cry and groan with pain we are not doing ourselves a favour, because we're wasting energy which we can ill afford. On the other hand, crying or groaning transmits a stronger message than talking.

TAP TIPPY TAP

TAPPITY TAP

Why do we dance?

No one can resist a dance. Watch the normally most miserable person listening to exciting music and, even if they're only tapping their feet, they are still dancing to the beat. Everyone has some rhythm, and primates are no exception. Chimpanzees perform a kind of ritual dance where they jump from tree to tree and tear up bits of earth for no apparent reason other than sheer enjoyment.

Dance is completely unlike other forms of motion. When we walk, run, jump, crawl, the purpose is to move from one place to another. With dance, there is no such intention. Instead, the purpose of dance is to take you out of yourself, to make you an actor and a dreamer.

A study of many folk dances from around the world shows that the dance is a drama of the various activities carried out in each society. These activities range from hunting and war to religious ceremonies and healing. The dance imitates the kind of movements that take place in each activity. War dances often include war cries, punching and spearing the air. They give an impression of the movements that might happen during a fight. The rhythm of the dance helps to bring people together so that they feel at one with the community around them.

This kind of folk-dancing is going out of fashion in cities and urban areas throughout the world. In these places, people often do not have much in common with those who live about them. The most popular forms of dancing in Western cities are ballroom dancing and disco-dancing. People dance alone, or in couples, rather than as a large group. The dances represent courtship or sexual advances. In the disco dances, for example, dancers frequently make gestures with sexual overtones, like swaying from side to side and wiggling the hips. The dancers occasionally turn away from each other then come together again, in a way that mimics the features of a relationship. Like other art forms, dance expresses human emotions. Each dance says something. Think of the dances you know. What do you think each one is trying to say?

Why do people scream at
rock concerts?

Elvis Presley, The Beatles, Bros, Michael Jackson, Wham. Whenever those stars appeared on stage a bout of screaming started. Hands reached forward, fists clenched and unclenched, hands grasped the head and tried to tear the hair out, faces looked as if they were in the most incredible pain, the screams rose to a crescendo – and that was before a single note was played.

A change of scene now. One member of that audience is walking down a quiet street on a quiet Sunday afternoon. She walks into her front room, and finds her favourite rock star having a cup of tea with her Mum and Dad. Of course, she would be incredibly surprised. She may be shy, excited, flushed and shocked all rolled into one but she would be very unlikely to scream.

Screaming is a signal that many mammals use when they experience pain and fear. It's an alarm call, more immediate than crying, that says that help is needed. Sometimes, people scream when they sense danger, alerting anyone nearby and, if they are threatened by an attack, warning the attacker not to come near them. So why do people scream at rock concerts when they don't appear to be in any danger?

In a concert, the scream indicates that the screamer feels an emotion that is as strong as pain. That emotion appears as a very strong message that teenagers fancy an idol so much they are unable to restrain themselves. When thousands are screaming at once, the effect is magnified. The sight of everyone else screaming causes a chain reaction, rather like panic. When someone panics, it frightens others around and the panic spreads. You may have seen this type of response in 'disaster' movies.

There is a disadvantage. If you go to one of these concerts you're bound to lose out: you can't hear the group because the audience is making all the noise!

Comforting Ourselves

*This section looks at the way
we behave towards ourselves when we need
a little care and attention.*

Why do we stroke our chins?

One way of helping someone who is unhappy is to give them a little cuddle or a caress. It certainly seems to work very well with crying babies. When we are troubled or in pain it helps if there is a person around who can reassure us. It works wonders when a friend pats us on the back or gives us a nice big hug.

On other occasions, when we are nervous, we tend to cuddle ourselves in various ways. We might rub our noses, scratch our heads, stroke our chins, interlock our hands or give ourselves a hug. We are simply comforting ourselves. Often, we don't even know we're doing it. When we're just plain bored, it can help to stroke our chin. It makes us feel better, we know that someone cares – even though it's only ourselves!

Why do we stroke cats?

There's nothing so cosy and relaxing as putting your pet kitten on your knee and listening to and feeling it purr as you stroke it. It does seem that cats like being stroked. It gives us pleasure too because it's a soothing and comforting thing to do and because we know we are making our cat happy. However, we may well be getting even more out of it than the cat.

Stroking is a kind of grooming action. We groom ourselves when we comb our hair or wash our faces. We are making ourselves look nice. Sometimes we take part in a social grooming. The best example is when girls plait each other's hair. This is a friendly act which is not seen very often among humans, but is a constant feature of life among hairy apes and monkeys. They are always stroking and picking fleas and mites off each other, and they really enjoy doing it.

Since we humans probably did a lot of social grooming in our far distant past, when our ancestors had much more hair over their entire body, it is not surprising that we still want to do a bit of grooming. Unfortunately, only our head offers us much hair to groom, and sometimes there's not too much of that. The cat is a very hairy animal, covered with lots of nice thick fur, so we can satisfy our ancient urges by stroking our cat.

Why do we chew gum?

We have different ways of expressing how we feel
even if we don't want others to know. For example,
we tend to rub our hands together when we're
nervous or anxious, and yawn when we're bored.
These are actions we do despite ourselves. We can't
help it. Even though we may try to pretend we're
very interested in listening to a professor tell us
about the feeding activity of the lesser-spotted
mugwump, in the end we can't stifle a big yawn.

So where does chewing gum come into all this?
Well, these activities are the kind of things we do
when we feel anxious. Some people can eat a
tremendous meal and continue to nibble because
it helps to divert attention from the way they really
feel. If we nibble lots of chocolate, nuts and crisps
we eventually become quite fat. Chewing gum is
the alternative. Instead of nibbling we can occupy
our mouth chewing. If it's the right type of gum,
it's healthy, we can chew the same piece for a long
time and we'll hardly put on any weight.

THHRRRRRP

Why Do We Make Faces?

*This section looks at the messages
we give when we pull faces.*

Why do we cock-a-snook?

Cocking-a-snook has been a popular form of insult for three hundred years. The tip of the thumb is held to the nose and the fingers are waggled about. The waggling fingers represent a cock's comb and a 'snook' is a sign of sneering. 'Thumbing your nose' is another way of describing this insult.

Why has this insult lasted so long? It seems that it started on the Continent and that it was a popular way of poking fun at the English who did not understand what it meant. People took great glee when the English thumbed their nose back thinking this was a polite form of greeting. Eventually, the insult crossed the Channel.

There are a number of reasons why this insult has been so effective. The waggling fingers and the upturned nose look rather like the aggressive comb of the fighting cock. This means the action is offensive and compares the insulted person to an animal. The nose is also the main feature of the face which is most laughed at. We often refer to beautiful eyes or a beautiful mouth but we don't talk much about the charms of the nose. We're more likely to say that person has a 'funny nose' like a pickled onion, perhaps, or a potato. A famous writer called Cyrano de Bergerac wrote a book called *The Nose* based on his experiences. He had a very long nose and people made fun of him but he must have cocked-a-snook back at them.

Why do we snarl?

Many thousands of years ago, before weapons were properly fashioned, humans would have fought with one of the most effective natural weapons — their teeth. Before the discovery of refined foods, teeth were a lot sharper and stronger than they are today. Where societies have a diet of natural, unprocessed food, their teeth are in much better condition than those societies that live on high-sugar, pre-packaged food.

Infants tend to use their teeth a lot more than adults. Often, infant teachers keep a wary look out for budding Draculas who may cause their class-mates serious harm through biting. For adult men, whose teeth have either fallen out or are stuffed with fillings, fists and elbows are more effective in a fight than teeth. Women tend to bite rather more than men, possibly because they are physically weaker, and teeth are easy to use.

Look at professional wrestlers sizing each other up. They always do a good deal of snarling with the teeth bared as the lips are drawn back. Adults who are furious with each other often snarl, too. Snarling does not necessarily mean that we intend biting. Snarlers frequently make the grunting noises and the baring of teeth movements but they do not usually bite. The movement may be a throwback to those early days when two angry humans got ready to use their big healthy teeth on each other. Now we have discovered artificial weapons, we are left with the gesture but we don't need the action.

Why is it rude to poke out your tongue?

'Don't be so rude, you nasty little creature.'
  'Why? I only poked out my tongue at that man.'
  'Exactly. It's very rude.'
  'But why is it rude, Daddy?'
  'It just is. Now, behave yourself.'
  It's a perfectly good question, though. Why *is* it rude to poke out a tongue? As babies, when we are given food we don't like, the automatic reaction is to push it away with the tongue. When small children, and even some adults, are concentrating very hard on something they often poke out their tongue very slightly when someone approaches. They are not doing this action purposely. It is a way of saying, 'I'm very busy at the moment. Please don't disturb me.'
  Poking out the tongue is an act of rejection. When we do it purposely it is a way of saying 'Keep away, I don't like you.' In this case, human beings seem to have taken the place of food.

The sticking-out tongue is a rude gesture amongst many peoples. Eritrean children, from East Africa, have a great difficulty in saying the sound 'th' because they feel it is rude to stick out their tongues.

Bodyspeak

*This section looks at the stories
our bodies tell.*

Why can you have a stiff upper lip?

Some people, for example soldiers, have an unspoken rule that they should not cry at distressing events like funerals. If they do break down they feel it's some kind of admission of weakness. If you try to hold yourself back from crying there are a number of signs that betray the way you feel. You shake and try to stifle the sobs. Even if you can stop shaking there is one sign that will give you away – your upper lip starts to quiver. If you can stop that then you've controlled yourself. Hence, the command: 'Keep a stiff upper lip!'

Have a go at keeping a stiff upper lip even when you're not upset. You may find it makes you laugh!

Why do we give the signs 'thumbs up' and 'thumbs down'?

Thumbs up. Good news. Thumbs down. You're for it. Why use those particular signs? Well, it seems that's another trick we picked up from the Romans.

In ancient Rome specially trained swordsmen, called gladiators, fought each other in special arenas. The crowds flocked to see these spectacles because they had a part to play in the outcome of the fight. At the end of the combat the winner would ask the crowd for a decision on the fate of his defeated rival. If most of the crowd made a stabbing movement downwards with their thumbs, the verdict was death. In other words, the gladiator was given the 'thumbs down'. The thumb was likely to be pointing down because the crowd were sitting on raised tiers above the arena and they pointed down at the gladiator. On the other hand, if the spectators thought the gladiator's life should be spared, they raised their hands with their thumbs covered up. That wasn't quite the same action as the 'thumbs up', but it has come down through history with the same meaning.

Through later centuries, 'thumbs up' came to mean OK, and 'thumbs down' the opposite. This is probably because an up movement signifies hope and happiness. A down movement seems to say we're 'down in the dumps'. The 'thumbs down' is an easy way of transmitting bad news from a distance, or letting you know something so another person can't see. Fortunately, it doesn't mean that someone is going to put you to death.

Why do we look down our noses?

What a snob! He looks down his nose at everyone. Tilt your head back and look down your nose at an object beneath you. You can't help looking like a snob if you do that.

People have always used their bodies to indicate social status. This originates from the earliest times when priests would throw themselves on the temple floor before gods. Courtiers would bow down before the god-like Pharaoh in ancient Egypt. Muslims have always knelt and prostrated themselves towards Mecca. Christians kneel before their God. We can see those actions in many instances today. Subjects of whatever class lower their bodies by bowing or curtseying before royalty.

Imagine you're in trouble with your head-teacher. If she stands glowering down at you then you feel at a distinct disadvantage. The act of looking up makes you feel uneasy, and from that position it becomes difficult to say what you think.

Some people are so used to bossing others about that they look down their noses without realizing it. One way of making yourself seem taller is to tilt back your head — an action bossy people do unconsciously. If you look at someone else from that position you'll find it very difficult to look anywhere other than straight down your nose!

Why do clothes speak?

The Bible tells us that Adam and Eve were the first people to wear clothes. This isn't exactly world-shattering news since Adam and Eve were supposed to be the first people. When they were in the Garden of Eden they were naked but they didn't bother about clothes. Only when that had sinned, after eating the apple on the Tree of Knowledge, did they realize they were naked.

To those of us who live in a cold climate we know that the Garden of Eden must have been in a warm part of the world otherwise Adam and Eve would have felt the need for clothes even before eating the apple. We wear clothes, primarily, to protect us from the weather. Even in hot weather, clothes are important. They protect our bodies from the harmful rays of the sun and, by trapping pockets of air, they keep us cool.

In Western societies, wearing clothes is an important social convention. It's considered indecent to walk around the streets naked even in very warm weather. There are other societies, in parts of South America and Africa, where nudity does not matter and people do not wear clothes. In Arab countries, it is customary for religious Muslim women to cover their entire body, including their faces, in black.

In most parts of the world, clothes are ornamental as well as protective. People develop a particular style depending on the part of the world where they live. Since the beginning of this century, communications have improved tremendously. This has meant that fashions have spread far and wide. The Indian sari, the Japanese kimono, the Morroccan fez, the Afghanistani kaftan, the Peruvian alpaca and American jeans are all examples of how different styles of clothing have become popular in parts of the world well away from where they were originally worn.

Clothes can reveal a lot about a person's social position. In ancient societies, the priest-kings and royalty wore special robes which made them stand out from the rest of the population. This still happens today. We can also make good guesses about what people do, their personality and their attitudes by looking at their clothes.

Some forms of clothing are closely connected with jobs. Astronauts, sportspeople, ice-packers, divers, miners, motor-cyclists, paratroopers and, of course, fashion models all wear clothes that are essential to the job they do. They can't do the job unless they wear those particular clothes. In other kinds of work, people wear clothes, as a uniform, to show that they do a particular job. That's true of nurses, bus-conductors, chefs, air-line pilots and many schoolchildren. Doctors, dentists and people working on science experiments frequently wear white coats. The coats protect them from splashed chemicals and grease but the white colour is now connected to science.

What about social class? Until quite recently, in Britain, it was quite easy to tell an individual's social class. Wealthy, upper-class people wore expensive and elaborate clothes of all sorts of colours. Working-class people were usually very poor and could not afford good quality clothes. They would wear cheaper clothes in drab colours. The middle classes wanted to dress like the ruling classes but they could not afford it. Instead, they wore suits and dresses that showed they did not work with their hands or do 'dirty work', like working-class people. The men wore suits and white shirts which showed they did 'clean' work. The women tended to dress in fabrics that were imitations of the clothes of the wealthier people.

Today, it's more difficult to tell who is rich and who is poor, who is upper-class and who is working-class. One reason is that many upper-class people are no longer so rich. Also, there has been a kind of swop in fashions. Manual workers often wear smart suits and dresses in the evenings and weekends to contrast with their daily working clothes. White collar workers tend to wear much more casual clothes out of working hours.

Jeans are worn throughout society, especially by young people, whatever their background. But there are giveaway signs. A wealthy person will often wear a gold-studded belt on his jeans to show that he has a lot of money despite his casual style of clothing.

Clothes are a good guide to personality. If you are really outgoing and bubbly you would tend to wear clothes that show the world how you feel.

Your clothes would probably be colourful and stylish, maybe outrageous. If you were quieter and preferred to be part of the background then you would tend to wear 'quieter' clothes so you would not draw attention to yourself.

And attitudes? Well, how can clothes say what we think? For a start they can suggest whether we conform or rebel. Someone who conforms will usually wear the same kinds of clothes as the people who try to set the standards for society like prime ministers, head teachers, archbishops and civil servants. Rebels' clothes usually indicate they don't agree with the social codes. Their clothes can cover a whole range of styles from the girl 'punk' with torn stockings to the man who wears a floral shirt with a conservative suit. Many younger people wear clothes that show they differ from their elders. The problem is that when enough people try to look different, they all end up looking the same!

Things to do

1 Do clothes influence what people think about you? Why not find out? Try to look as scruffy as possible then visit the bus station, airport or railway station where there are plenty of people. Ask twenty different people the time and note their reasons. Tick a category below for each person:

Polite:

Smiled:

Hardly noticed me:

Hostile:

On another day go to the same place looking as smart as possible and ask a sample of twenty different people the same question. Tick each category as you did before.

2 Observe carefully the people about you. Make a careful note of their clothes. Do the clothes tell you anything about their character or their occupation?

Why do body movements say things?

Imagine you have just heard some really good news. You have won a dream holiday to a sun-kissed island in the Caribbean. You'll be jumping for joy and there'll be a real spring in your step. If you had just found out you'd failed an important examination then you'd be slumped in a chair with your head hanging in utter dejection.

Most people don't have to tell you how they feel, you can see it in their walk and posture. A young person strides along the road head held high. She is transmitting the message that she is feeling happy. The position of the head is a useful pointer towards people's inner feelings. It is very difficult to keep your 'chin up' when things are going against you.

Think of your teachers, those that move around a lot and those that keep absolutely still. You must have come across the 'pacers', those teachers that move up and down the classroom without pause. It may be that they're just fidgety but the 'pacers' could also be expressing the desire to get out beyond the walls of the classroom. A 'pacer' may simply be a failed adventurer, someone who's exploring the world within the classroom.

Lack of movement can also tell you a lot about a person. What about the teacher who stands absolutely still, barely twitching a muscle? You may see similar postures on TV during a royal ceremony. In any culture, you can often recognize the individuals with the highest status. They remain motionless whilst everyone else has to scurry around for them.

Some groups move in characteristic ways. Some groups of people tend to move their hands a lot more when speaking, others may move with a certain rhythm as if music plays in their blood. Movement can also reflect social class. People of a military background tend to walk rather stiffly with shoulders thrown back and head held high as if they were playing at being soldiers. People who are down and out usually trudge along slowly with their shoulders hunched.

Finally, there are some forms of movement that you can't mistake. Imagine someone swaying to and fro as they stagger along the pavement. Their legs don't seem to agree with each other and they always seem in danger of collapsing. You're right, of course, they've just been drowning their sorrows with spirit, or, maybe, they're very spirited actors just pretending to be drunk.

Things to do

1 Do actions speak louder than words? Imagine you are in a country where you cannot speak the language. Suppose you wanted to express the following. What gestures and movements would you use? Try this out with a friend and see if they can interpret your body language.

a I'm lost!
b Where's the nearest train station?
c I don't understand.
d I'm fed up.
e I'm feeling really good.
f It's much too hot.
g It's much too cold.
h I'm feeling sick.
i I've lost all my money
j I feel completely at home here.

2 Look at these drawings. What is each posture saying?

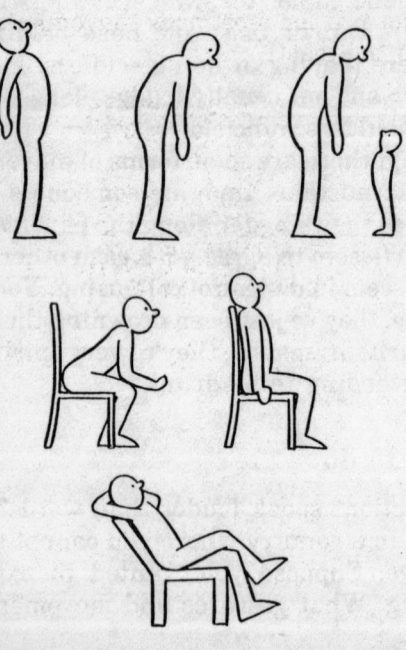

3 Watch a play on TV with the sound turned down completely. Look carefully at the body movements of the participants. Can you work out what they are saying? If you have a video you could play a game with friends by interpreting the body language and seeing who gets closest to what is actually said.

4 Try and see as many films or programmes as possible featuring people of different nationalities and from different cultures. Are there differences in the extent to which body movements are used to express meaning? Note down all the movements you can; for example, shoulder shrugs, chest puffing, hand and arm movements. Make a league table of the nationalities or cultures starting from those that use the most body movements to those that use the least.

Help!

This section looks at how our bodies behave when we're frightened and whether we can get over our fears.

Why do we get butterflies?

We have all had that fluttering feeling in our stomach called 'butterflies'. It comes on us at times when we are very tense or frightened. Children who have been naughty feel it just before a strict teacher confronts them. Many people have butterflies before they take an exam. We may have them before taking off in an aeroplane or looking down from a very high building, I experience 'butterflies' just before I go down a steep hill in a very fast car.

This strange sensation comes about when our body alarm system gets to work. Our brain receives a message from our senses that danger threatens and the brain transmits messages all over the body preparing us for action. The brain needs a lot of energy to do all this work. Consequently, a lot of blood carrying food and oxygen is diverted to the brain from places where it is not really needed. One place that does not need a rich supply of blood at this time is the stomach. As the blood surges away from the stomach towards the brain we experience that sinking feeling of 'butterflies'.

Why do weight-lifters spit on their hands?

When we come across surprising and unpleasant situations, our body prepares to meet the shock. The heart beats faster, the hair 'stands on end' and we sweat. In hot weather, certain parts of our body sweat more than others – the forehead, neck and armpits. We also sweat when we are shocked because our body heats up as we produce extra energy to meet the disturbance. Sweating helps to get rid of the extra heat. What is strange about this emotional sweating is that it also takes place in the palms of our hands and the soles of our feet which do not sweat in hot weather. See for yourself next time you get an unpleasant surprise.

Sweating lubricates the surface of the palms so that we can grapple better with the real or imaginary enemy. In cricket, look at a bowler preparing to bowl. He spits on his hands so they can grip the ball better. Weight-lifters do the same before they lift their weights. It looks as if we have learned to imitate our body's responses in activities that demand extra energy resources. We have learned a lesson from ourselves!

Why does our hair stand on end?

'I got such a fright my hair stood on end.' Look at comics like *The Dandy* and *Beano*, and you'll see that when the characters get a shock, their hair stands on end like the bristles on a stiff broom. In real life this does not happen in quite the same way.

Come out of a hot bath into a cold room and goose pimples will start to show on your skin. Goose pimples occur when the muscles in the skin at the base of the hair contract causing the hairs to stand on end. As a result, the hairs trap layers of air which prevent the heat escaping from our bodies.

When our hair stands on end, air is trapped and our body keeps warm. This is a very useful response if we have had a fright or a shock. During this time, the hormone adrenaline in our bodies gets to work. Adrenaline is a chemical that our body produces in response to stress. It makes the heart pump blood a lot faster around the body and puts us in a state of general readiness for any effort we have to make.

For many mammals, such as monkeys, baboons and apes, this response has an additional purpose. When a baboon wishes to scare a potential enemy, its hair stands on end giving the impression it is much larger and more frightening than it really is. This type of threat display is useless in humans because we hardly have any hair. We wouldn't seem much bigger if all our hair stood on end so it's not much use as a frightener.

We can make ourselves bigger in other ways: drawing ourselves to our full height or puffing our chests out. Our hair may well stand on end when we face a potential enemy but it serves to conserve our energy rather than to scare off our enemies.

Why can we unlearn some fears?

Many people have fears where there is no real cause because the thing they fear won't physically harm them. Many people go into screaming hysterics if they so much as catch a glimpse of a harmless spider or snake. One man who was terrified of thunder listened to every single weather forecast he could. He travelled miles away from his home area if there was a threat of thunder there. One woman was so frightened of the tiniest bit of dirt that she had to scrub her house the whole day.

Many fears are perfectly understandable. We should be afraid of going near a raging fire because the fire will hurt us. We learn to avoid such dangers, but there are some things that we do not need to learn. An experiment was carried out on babies by taking them to the edge of a drop covered by glass. The babies were unable to crawl across the drop even though they would have been perfectly safe. They could not see the glass and had an innate fear of falling.

How can we unlearn the irrational fears? One way is to discover that the things we fear cannot really do us much harm. A person can be gradually encouraged to face their fears. This kind of treatment is practised by trained nurses and doctors. Imagine Mr Jones who is terrified of spiders. The nurse puts a tiny spider in a sealed glass jar in one corner of the room. She leads Mr Jones into the room. Mr Jones sees the spider and quakes in terror. The nurse feels his sweaty hand and tries to soothe him. She might also call the spider a friendly name. Mr Jones calms down but he is still quite frightened when he leaves the room a few minutes later.

Mr Jones returns the next week and gains confidence when he is in the same room as the spider. After a few months of constant encouragement from the nurse he can even approach the glass jar containing the spider. On the following occasion the nurse puts a slightly bigger spider in the glass jar. After this, Mr Jones can even enter the room by himself. There comes a time when Mr Jones can take the spider home and he learns to touch the spider. Within two years, Mr Jones has half a dozen large furry tarantulas trotting around his table. The treatment has worked. Mr Jones loves spiders . . . but he goes into a dead faint whenever he sees a human being!

Things to do

Carry out a survey on fears. Ask people to list their five greatest fears. What fear crops up the most? Which fears are rational and which fears do you think are irrational?

Who Loves Ya, Baby?
Who Hates Ya?

*This section looks at how we behave
towards the animals we love . . . and animals
we hate.*

Why do we love pandas?

One of human beings' favourite animals is the panda. Other favourites are monkeys, chimpanzees and gorillas, as well as cats and dogs. Thinking about it, these are rather strange choices. Apart from in zoos, most of us don't come across pandas and chimpanzees very often. We don't see them trotting up and down the street like cats and dogs, or snuggling up on the cosiest chair in the household.

There aren't many pandas left wild on Earth, and most of those that are left are found in remote forests in China. Again, most gorillas are found in the jungle of East Africa, and whilst chimpanzees and monkeys are a little more widespread, Europeans would have to travel across one continent at least before they can see one in the wild.

Pandas, monkeys, chimpanzees and gorillas do have something in common. They're a bit like humans. They all have facial expressions, however limited, that can express the mood they're in. They can all stand erect like humans and they can use their forelimbs to feed or throw stones or swing

72

about from tree to tree. With their wide eyes and their mournful expressions the pandas are a particular favourite because those are precisely the type of expressions that draw adult humans towards babies. Their cuddly fur must be an added attraction.

We tend to be drawn to cats and dogs when they do things that mimic us. A cat appeared on a TV commercial for cat food where it dug its foot into a tin, like a spoon, to scoop out the meaty chunks. This cat was a great favourite with TV audiences because of this little trick. There have been programmes about dogs that jump about when a certain football team appears on TV and cats that seem to be avid fans of table tennis. The more human the moods the pet shows the more we are attracted towards them.

Things to do

Does this explanation hold for your, and your friends', favourite animals? Test it out. Ask your friends in school to list their five favourite animals in order of preference. Then allocate five points to animal number 1, four points to animal number 2, and so on until you come to the fifth favourite which receives 1 point. For example, Lisa makes her choice:

1 Panda
2 Horse
3 Cat
4 Monkey
5 Chimpanzee.

73

And Abdul makes his list:

1 Dog
2 Zebra
3 Dolphin
4 Chimpanzee
5 Panda

The panda would have 6 points, (5 from Lisa and 1 from Abdul), the horse would have 4 (from Lisa only), the cat would have 3 (Lisa only), the monkey would have 2 (Lisa only), the chimpanzee would have 3 (1 from Lisa and 2 from Abdul), the dog would have 5 (Abdul only) and so on. Take a list from at least 30 friends then tot up the points.

How do the sexes differ? Do girls seem to prefer one animal more than boys? Do younger children prefer some animals more than others? And adults? Do they differ from children? Do we prefer animals that behave like humans?

Why do we have pet hates?

There's a picture that's always cropping up in comic books. It's of a mischievous boy or girl holding out the palm of their hand. On it sits a harmless little mouse. The owner has a wicked smile because everyone else is jumping on chairs and their hair is standing on end with shock and fear. Now if you could ask the mouse, it would probably squeak with amazement at all the terror it caused.

How can a tiny animal inspire such fear? Not only mice but frogs, snakes and spiders seem more terrifying than a lion, tiger or even a dragon. Why do these small animals terrify us? After all, they can't hurt us physically. We must look like huge monsters to a mouse.

One explanation is that it is a fear inherited through hundreds of generations. There are poisonous toads, snakes and spiders; and mice can spread disease. Our early ancestors would have come across these nasty and dangerous creatures, which are very different from those we know in our home and back garden. Could their horror have remained a human fear through so many generations? Today, many people claim they hate snakes because they are poisonous. Yet the chance of being killed by a poisonous snake in Britain is 1 in 500,000,000. In other words, one person in every 100 years is likely to die of a snake bite in Britain.

And what about frogs, spiders and mice? The main complaints are:

'Frogs? Ugh! It's their slimy skin.'
'We hate spiders because they have so many legs.'
'Mice scuttle along in a horrible way.'

Things to do

1 Whatever the reason we do have strong feelings about these beasties. What are your friends' pet hates? Here's an opportunity to do your own investigation into slimy frogs and creepy-crawlies. Make a league table of pet hates. Ask 50 people what three animals they hate most, putting the nastiest first. Ask them why they hate these animals so much.

2 Often people differ in their pet hates according to age. When you ask people about their pet hates check their age group. Split the age groups into:
Under 10
10 to 20
over 20

You'll love finding out about people's hates.

Keeping Together

This section looks at how we behave when we want to keep in with friends, parents and neighbours.

Why do we follow our mothers?

A famous German biologist called Konrad Lorenz discovered, earlier this century, that he had become the mother of a group of small chicks. He wasn't the real mother, of course, but the chicks treated him just like one. They followed him wherever he went.

Lorenz went on to investigate this strange happening. Why should the chicks follow him, and not other hens? It seems that the chicks became attached to the first thing they saw after hatching which, in this case, was a human being.

Lorenz gave a name to this happening; he called it 'imprinting'. It is thought that imprinting may also take place with human beings.

Experiments have been carried out with babies of one or two days old that point to their looking towards their own mother rather than a stranger. Also, very young infants can learn to recognize certain smells and it may be that they learn their mother's smell at quite an early age.

No one, though, has seen a group of human babies toddling off after a great big chicken!

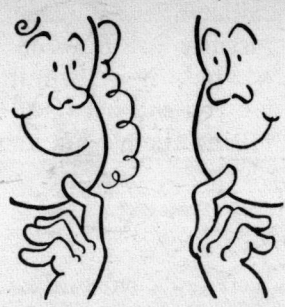

Why are friends copy cats?

Usually, we are relaxed with our friends. We want them to join in our activities, and we expect to join in theirs. We play games with friends, we sunbathe with them, we eat with them; often we have similar outlooks on the world. Friends even yawn together.

When people are comfortable in each other's company they often copy each other without realizing what they're doing. If one person decides to cup her chin in her hand when chatting to a friend then, sooner or later, the friend adopts the same position. There are lots of examples you may have come across: two old men leaning on a gate together, women talking to each other with their arms folded, one person nodding and others nodding in agreement, a group of boys standing at a street corner with their hands in their pockets.

These actions are called posture echoes. It means that when one person takes up a stance, like putting their hands in their pockets, the friend they are with will often do the same thing. It is a subconscious way of showing friendship. They are close because they are doing the same thing. People who are uncomfortable with each other do not do this, their bodily postures are different.

So, there's a whole new meaning to the word 'copy-cat'. When you call boys and girls copy-cats you're really telling them what good friends they are.

Things to do

1 Watch your friends carefully when they are together. Take a mental note of any actions like crossing the hands, scratching heads, stroking cheeks, rubbing noses, hands in pockets, leaning forward, leaning backwards, any bodily movement you can describe. Do friends copy each other? What bodily actions are most easily copied? What happens when strangers meet?

2 Scratch your head in front of some friends and see if they copy. The best copy-cat should be your best friend!

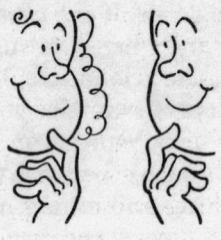

Why do we gossip?

'Pssst, John. Did you hear about Mandy? She's supposed to be going out with Akhtar but last night I saw her at the pictures with Lloyd and they were kissing each other in the back row. Promise not to tell!'

'You know the man next door? He's strange, isn't he? He never says anything to anybody. I always see him going out last thing at night. I wonder where he goes. You never know with those quiet 'uns, do you?'

'I see the Joneses have bought a brand new car. Beats me where they get the money from. Wouldn't surprise me if they've been up to a bit of no good.'

Yes, that's all gossip, a very popular pastime. Newspapers have even built an industry around it. There are gossip columnists and gossip magazines which attract many readers. In the press, this gossip is usually about well-known people such as royalty and soap-opera stars but there is also gossip that is much more widespread, as many of us know to our cost. It's not very pleasant when people talk about us behind our backs.

If anyone does anything slightly unusual it attracts gossip. Unusual or strange activities threaten our sense of security. This is because they are different and we are not sure how to respond to them. If a girl goes out with a boy other than her regular boy-friend onlookers may talk about it because they wouldn't like it to happen to them. People tend to be worried by quiet people who keep themselves to themselves, and there's always a bit of jealousy when someone buys a car which is better than yours. Children who don't mix with other children at school are usually the butt of gossip because most children tend to go around in groups and they can't understand loners.

In many small communities around the world, from Australian suburbs to Spanish hamlets, gossip controls the people who live there. People who live in big cities don't have to worry too much about the gossip of their neighbours. They don't have to mix with them and can avoid seeing them for a long time so that the gossip dies down. That is not true of small communities where you see the same people each day. Life is a lot better if you can avoid being unpopular there.

In many villages, particularly in southern Europe, people gossip so that everyone knows everyone else's business and there's no room for nosy-parkering. Householders are unwilling to allow strangers in when other villagers are looking in case this arouses gossip. So villagers are encouraged to behave like everybody else.

When you next hear all those tongues wagging remind yourself that it is probably just a bit of innocent social control.

Things to think about

Does gossip go on at your school? Is it usually about one particular person? How do people who are gossiped about respond? Do they become part of the group or do they become more isolated? Do you think gossip might be a pressure on people to behave like everyone else?

Expressions

*This section looks at the many expressions
used to describe the way we behave.*

Why are we on tenterhooks?

You're at the airport waiting to meet a penfriend. You've corresponded with this friend for years but you've never met. On the arrival board you've seen that the aeroplane has arrived. It won't be long now before she enters the arrival hall. . . .

Two minutes until the end of the Wembley Cup Final. The score is 2–2. Your team has just been awarded a penalty. Your favourite player runs up to take the kick. . . .

These are examples of instances when you might be on tenterhooks. Your nerves are on edge, the suspense is more than you can take. What has all this got to do with tenterhooks?

Tenterhooks made their first appearance in the cloth-making industry. When the cloth had to be fully stretched it was pulled on a machine called a tenter and held in place by tenterhooks. So, like the cloth, when you're on tenterhooks you're under a lot of strain.

Why do we laugh up a sleeve?

Up your sleeve? It's a strange place to laugh. Given the tight fit of present-day sleeves, you could barely breathe up them, let alone have a good laugh. 'Laughing up your sleeve' is an expression that means you are trying to hide your laughter from the person you're laughing at. But why a sleeve? Wouldn't it be easier to hide your laugh in a jacket or a hat or even an umbrella?

For the answer to the riddle we have to go back a long time – the sixteenth century – when the nobility in the English royal court wore loose sleeved garments in which they could hide their expressions. If you were at a solemn court occasion and you suddenly felt like giggling, then you could protect yourself by laughing up your sleeve.

Today, the loose sleeves have gone but the expression remains. Mind you, the sleeves could make a return. It would be nice to have a big loose sleeve we could laugh up when we have a fit of the giggles.

Why do we ride hobby horses?

When someone is on their hobby horse it means that they're on to their favourite subject. Everyone else might as well go to sleep because it will be ages before they stop talking. But what is a hobby horse?

The hobby horse was first seen in England in the seventeenth century. It was a kind of box on wheels on which the rider sat and pushed himself along, a forerunner of the bicycle. It must have been quite a pleasant occupation because it gives us the word 'hobby', meaning an enjoyable pastime.

Hobby horsing must have taken off in a big way in those days because a number of writers commented that people were free to ride their hobby horses as long as they didn't interfere with anyone else. Perhaps the effect of lots of hobby horses on the streets must have been a bit like noisy motorcyclists on a quiet Sunday afternoon. Today, we feel that people can amuse themselves with their pet subject, or their hobby horse, as long as they don't go on about it for too long.

Why do we weep crocodile tears?

Crocodiles weep as they open their great jaws to gobble up their victims. It may seem comforting that the crocodile who's having you for dinner cares so much that it's prepared to shed tears. In fact, the croc couldn't care less. When crocodiles open their jaws they shed tears as a reflex action just as we humans might drop a tear or two when specks of dust settle in our eyes.

Suppose you're behind someone you know in a queue for tickets for a popular concert. She gets the last ticket, so you are left without one. Turning round to you, she says: 'What a pity. It's not going to be any fun going without you,' and you know that she couldn't care less! Your friend is weeping crocodile tears because her words don't mean anything.

Another example of crocodile tears is someone who cries a lot for show. They shed buckets of tears for people for whom they care nothing.

Crocodiles probably weep a lot more than humans. They live longer than us and they enjoy their food; so, during an average life-time, a crocodile sheds a great many tears.

Why do we talk gibberish?

If someone manages to confuse you, there's a very good chance they're talking gibberish. The strange thing about gibberish is that it's named after an alchemist and philosopher called Geber who talked anything but gibberish. Geber, who was thought to have been born in Iraq and to have had his home in Baghdad, was an Arab who lived in the eleventh century. His scientific ideas threatened the authority of the rulers at that time and he had to keep his work secret.

To overcome this problem, Geber decided to write in code. Anyone reading Geber's work would have thought it a lot of nonsense and would have taken no notice of it. Of course, Geber and a few close friends would have understood his writings but to anyone else it was just a load of 'Geberish'.

Why do we send people to Coventry?

Suppose you have done something very unpopular like telling a tale about a friend. Your friends may gather together and refuse to speak to you: they're sending you to Coventry.

This expression had its origin in the English Civil War, between 1642 and 1646, when the Royalists were fighting the Parliamentarians. When Royalist prisoners were captured in Birmingham they were sent to nearby Coventry, where they were imprisoned. Coventry was a Parliamentary stronghold, so the Royalist prisoners were very unpopular and no one in the town would speak to them. They really were sent to Coventry!

Why do we boycott somewhere?

When we boycott a shop or a restaurant, it means that we refuse to buy goods from it, usually because of some action on the part of the owner. It may be that the owner has raised the prices too high or he may have treated his employees very badly.

The first person to be 'boycotted' was a Captain Charles Boycott who was a rent collector in County Mayo, Ireland, in the nineteenth century. After a bad harvest, the tenants were very poor and could not pay their rents. Captain Boycott was very severe and impatient. He refused to help them. Instead he ordered their eviction. His action was so nasty that even his own servants refused to stay with him and no one would work for him in their place. The only good thing that could be said of him is that he gave his name to the first Boycott!

Why can something be beyond the pale?

When you have done something 'beyond the pale'
it means that you have acted in a way that is completely unacceptable. The word 'pale' comes from
the Latin word *'palus'* which means a 'stake'. In
the 14th century, when the British armies settled
abroad they used stakes to mark the boundary
between themselves and the surrounding peoples
who they regarded as uncivilized. These people
were 'beyond the pale' and not acceptable as
company amongst the snobbish British.

Next time someone does you a bad turn, hold out
your stake and tell them to go 'beyond the pale'!

Superstitious?

This section looks at where superstitions come from and why we behave superstitiously.

Why do we bless a sneeze?

'Atishoo!'

'Bless you.'

'Thank you.'

That's the usual exchange after a sneeze. But why bless someone for sneezing?

One explanation is that the sneeze was thought to be a little explosion in the head of the sneezer. This was interpreted as a sign from the gods foretelling good or warning of evil. When a friend said 'Bless you' it would help the gods decide in your favour. Another explanation is that blessing would help restore the spirit to the sneezer because part of it might be lost in the explosion. This might explain why you cover your nose when you sneeze. Never mind the germs you are spreading – you're actually catching your spirit!

Why are black cats lucky?

If a black cat crosses your path then, tradition has it, your luck will change for the better. Whether this is true or not, the superstition about cats and luck has persisted for thousands of years.

The ancient Egyptians revered and worshipped the cat as a holy animal. In the cold northern climes of Scandinavia, Freya, the Scandinavian goddess of love, had her chariots drawn by cats.

The black cat has become the symbol of good fortune in Britain but if Belgians were to pass a black cat they wouldn't be as happy about it. In Belgium, Spain and the USA, the white cat brings good luck whereas the black cat indicates misfortune. They ought to carry a pot of white paint when they visit Britain — just in case!

Why is salt a sign of good luck?

Until recent times salt was associated with good things. Someone who is the 'salt of the earth' is a genuine, wonderful person who is trustworthy and reliable. Throwing salt over your left shoulder is a way of averting misfortune. Salt is an essential foodstuff but we now know that too much in our diet can lead to high blood pressure.

The reason why salt signifies good luck comes from the fact that it can be used to preserve food from decay. It became a symbol of everlasting life in ancient times and was used against all forces of evil.

The custom of throwing salt over the left shoulder originates from a tradition in Yorkshire. If you spilt any salt it was a sign of bad luck but you could remedy the accident by throwing a few grains of salt over your left shoulder.

Why do we touch wood?

'This is a marvellous little car. I've never had any trouble with it, touch wood.' It seems a strange thing to do. When people make a little boast about their good fortune they say 'touch wood', and desperately scrabble around for a piece of wood to touch. The person who boasts about his car says 'touch wood' to ensure that the car doesn't break down next day. He is not really going to stop the car breaking down, it's just a superstition.

There are a number of possible sources for the superstition, but there are two main explanations. The wood may refer to the bark of the oak tree which was considered a sacred tree by many pagan groups. Touching the oak tree helped to calm down the Norse god Thor if he was angry, and ensured his protection. The other explanation, which is Christian in origin, points to the wood as the material of the True Cross. In this case, the symbol of the Cross gives protection.

Next time you make a boast or you're relying on a piece of good luck, remember to take a piece of oak wood with you. On the other hand, it's only a superstition . . .

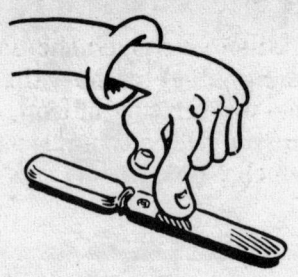

Why do we touch iron for good luck?

There is an ancient superstition that touching iron brings good luck, and some young children still reach out to touch the blade of a knife to ensure luck goes their way. The origins of this superstition do not rely as heavily on the gods as many others; they show some faith in humanity's powers of invention.

Until 1400 BC iron was known about, but it was regarded as a special metal, rather like gold or platinum today. Iron was first extracted in large quantities in Asia Minor by heating iron-containing rocks with charcoal. Until that time, bronze, a mixture of copper and tin, had been the main metal used for vessels and weapons. Iron is a much stronger metal than bronze and gave its discoverers an immediate advantage over those peoples still using bronze. Bronze weapons were no match for iron weapons. As a result, the Iron Age replaced the Bronze Age. To possess iron was associated with good fortune. The Hittites first extracted iron and they became very powerful in Western Asia at that time.

Of course, when you touch the blade of a knife you're touching steel rather than pure iron. Stainless steel is a mixture of iron, carbon, nickel and chromium but that all sounds a real mouthful, so we just touch iron!

Learning and Remembering

This section looks at how we can direct our behaviour to better learning and better remembering.

Why do we play games?

Hide-and-seek, Monopoly, cops and robbers, tiddlywinks, hopscotch, netball, chess, beggar-my-neighbour, snooker, football, musical chairs and Ludo – all are games played from childhood to adulthood. Adults like to pretend that they're too grown-up to play children's games, so they play adult games which they think children won't understand. Most adults think of Monopoly and tiddlywinks as children's games, but there are international events which bring together grown-ups from all over the world to decide who will be the world tiddlywinks champion or the grand champion of Monopoly.

Most games are played by adults and children. Sports like football and netball are first played by children, some of whom reach a very high standard in their late teens and twenties. Hide-and-seek and cops and robbers seem to be favoured by children, but adults often play cops and robbers for real!

Games are derived from spheres of human activity. People who study human behaviour are called social or human behaviourists and they promote the idea that games have a role in preparing children for adult life. In hide-and-seek you could be learning to avoid people who are looking for you like the tax inspector. Cops and robbers could be a game in which you are learning right from wrong, though some games have bad cops and good robbers.

Sports come into a different category. It is thought that some sports are modern versions of hunting. In some tribes today, it is still necessary to hunt animals for food. For those of us meat eaters who live in a more technological world, there is no need to go out and hunt because we can buy food in a shop. That means that there is no longer the traditional role of hunter. Instead, games as different as tiddlywinks and football are possibly hunting substitutes. Many of the same skills are used in sports and in hunting and victory in either brings the same sense of achievement. Footballers, for example, may see the opposing side as an animal which they must stalk and outwit in order to score a goal.

Why can we be good and bad at maths?

If you have ever been to a fair or a fête, then you have probably come across the 'Guess the Weight of the Cake' game. It's a difficult game to win.

Estimating numbers depends on what you're used to. Recently, I was at a football match with a friend who told me there were about twenty-five thousand people at the match. He was right. If he had said five thousand or ninety thousand I would have believed him, because I rarely go to football matches and I'm not used to estimating the size of a crowd. My friend goes every week.

About twenty years ago, a group of people in West Africa, the Kpelle, did an 'intelligence test' alongside a number of Americans. In one test both groups were asked to sort a number of cards containing two or five, red or green triangles or squares. They were asked to sort the cards in three different ways. The Americans did the test very quickly with no problems. The cards could be organized according to number, colour or shape.

The Kpelle had a great deal of difficulty with the test; some didn't have a clue how to do it.

By the standards of that test the Americans were intelligent and the Kpelle were not. Another test was set. This time the task was to estimate the number of cups it would take to scoop all the rice out of a bowl. In this test the Kpelle proved to be the experts whilst the Americans were hopeless.

Doing things you're good at depends on your background, education, culture and language as well as on natural talents. The Americans were more used to sorting out shapes whilst the Kpelle were much more experienced at estimating quantities of food. You learn skills through practice. Sometimes, we can mistake someone for being stupid just because they lack practice at performing a particular task. Their upbringing may mean that they can do very many things well that we find difficult but they cannot do the kinds of everyday tasks we carry out in our own group.

Things to do

Everyone has strengths and weaknesses. There is a story about Isaac Newton, one of the greatest geniuses of seventeenth-century Europe. He had two cats, an adult cat and a kitten. He didn't want to open the door each time a cat wanted to go out or come in; he was probably too busy with his scientific experiments. To solve the problem, Newton drilled two holes in his door – a big hole for the adult cat and a small one for the kitten. He failed to realize that the kitten could pass through the big hole as well.

Teachers, psychologists and employers all look for the best points in people and try to draw them out. How good are you at detecting strengths and weaknesses? Take ten people you know most and list all their best points and their weaknesses. Do they agree with you? Can you spot your own good and bad points? Would your friends agree with you about them?

ROYGBIV!

Why are mnemonics so useful?

Mnemonics? What are they, you'll ask yourself. 'Mnemonics' is a Greek word which is taken from Mnemosyne, a Goddess who was said to know everything. The word means a way of improving your memory.

Suppose we take the colours of the spectrum — that is, Red, Orange, Yellow, Green, Blue, Indigo, Violet. It would take some time to memorize those colours. Instead, think of the jingle: Richard Of York Gave Battle In Vain. The initials of each word are the same as those of the spectrum.

Another example is the chemical equation: ACID + BASE $\longrightarrow$ SALT + WATER. I use the phrase: All Bells Sound Well.

Whenever you need to learn something, it will be useful to make up little rhymes or phrases to help you to retain the information more easily. Who knows? Like Mnemosyne, you may end up knowing everything!

Why is it important to forget?

Imagine sitting in your class staring into thin air whilst all your class mates are busy writing away. Your teacher asks you to get on with your work. You say: 'I don't have to. I can remember it all anyway.' 'All right,' your teacher says, 'What did I say five minutes ago?' To his surprise, you repeat everything you've heard in the last ten minutes. The teacher gapes at you in astonishment. And you continue to stare out of the window.

Sounds incredible? Well, early this century there was a man who *did* remember everything. Like Superman, he was a journalist. He was a Russian called Solomon Veniaminoff. One day his editor told him off for going to an important event without a pen or paper. Veniaminoff simply sat down and wrote everything he had seen and heard. Veniaminoff became famous because of his remarkable memory. Unfortunately, he didn't have a very happy life. It can be a handicap to remember everything, just as it's a nuisance to forget everything.

Our memories are not perfect because we don't need to remember everything. Our memory is selective. We don't have to remember the telephone numbers of our friends because we can always look up the number in a telephone book. If we remembered every trivial event in our lives, our minds would become so cluttered that it would be impossible to sort out important details. With our faulty memories, we are probably much happier than Solomon Veniaminoff – the man who could never forget.

Left and Right

This section looks at whether we are left- or right-sided and what this tells us about ourselves.

Why do mothers usually hold their babies on their left side?

Even tiny babies are music fans: they like the rhythm and the beat. How do we know? Well, it seems nine out of ten babies prefer the left sides of their mothers. There they are cradled beside the heart whose regular beat has a very soothing effect. The sound of the beating heart stops babies crying and it makes them go to sleep more quickly. Many experiments have been carried out that show that babies who are played recorded heart beats are more settled.

What do mothers have to do with this? It seems that the vast majority hold their babies on the left side of their bodies so the baby's ear is near the heart. Most mothers do not mean to hold their babies there, it is just an instinct. One explanation could be that the mother unconsciously realizes that her baby is more settled when held on the left-hand side, and continues to do it because she remembers it is a more comfortable position. It could also be an inborn reaction like blinking or biting our nails – mothers hold their babies on the left because it feels natural to them.

Perhaps more mothers hold their babies near the heart because they use their left arm to cradle the baby and that leaves the right hand free to do things. Since many more women are right-handed than left-handed, it makes sense that babies tend to be held on the left. But most left-handed women hold their babies on the left-hand side even though it would be more convenient to hold them on their right side.

A baby develops in its mother's womb listening to and feeling her heartbeat. When it is born the world is a pretty frightening place. The baby recognizes the familiar heart-beat that it felt and heard in the womb, and it feels happier; and in turn, so does the mother.

What does all this have to do with buttons? See 'Why do girls button their coats. . . ?' below.

Why do girls button their coats on a different side from boys?

Even a little object like a button tells us a tremendous amount about the history of human behaviour. If you're a female take a look at your jacket or coat.

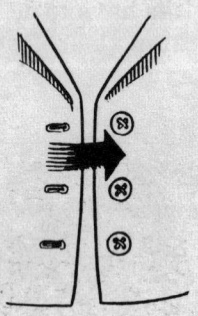

The chances are that it buttons right over left (*see diagram*). If you're a male, you'll find that the opposite holds true. Yet there is nothing in the male or female anatomy that would explain this difference. Clothes have been made in this way for many hundreds of years. It is curious that the tradition has persisted for so long but there is an explanation.

The reason for the female form of buttoning could still hold true today. Most mothers tend to hold their babies to their left breasts. The heart is on the left side of the body, near the left breast, and it is thought that the sound of the heart-beat is soothing and calms the baby. When women wore long garments it was more convenient to wrap the longer right side of the coat over their babies to keep them warm.

Men used to hold their weapons in their right hands – or most of them did since most of them were, and are, right-handed. In the days before pockets they used to warm their hands inside the fold of their coats to keep them warm. For the right-handed man this means that the left side of the coat must be wrapped over the right. The weapons have gone but the coat buttons remain.

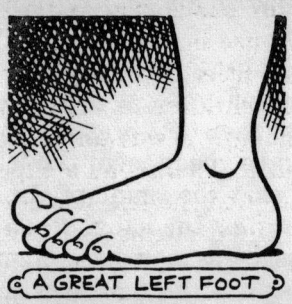

A GREAT LEFT FOOT

Why is there a side to your brain?

We know that hands are pretty useful. There's not much we can do without them. It's funny, though, that most of us use one hand more than the other. We are either right-handed or left-handed. Some lucky people have the best of both worlds because they use both hands equally well. They are called by a special name. We say they are 'ambidextrous'.

We don't just have a favourite hand. There's a favourite foot as well. The other day I heard a football commentator praise a player because he had a great left foot. Good left-footers are a great advantage to a team. Most right-handed people kick with their right foot and left-handers are usually left-footed.

No one teaches us which hand to use. One hand simply becomes the stronger. But we can learn to use the weaker hand. It's particularly useful if we injure our stronger hand.

Why do we use one part of our body more than another? The answer lies in our brain. One part of our brain controls the right side of our body and another part controls the left. It seems that one

118

part of the brain is in charge and makes itself felt in the way we use our hands and feet.

Until the twentieth century, parents used to encourage their children to write with their right hand. They thought it was unnatural and wrong to be left-handed. There was a superstition that the Devil controlled the left side of the body. The Latin word *sinistra* means 'left' but the English word 'sinister' means 'evil-threatening'. However, there's absolutely no proof that left-handers are more devilish than right-handers!

There is evidence that certain qualities are linked to right- or left-handedness. Left-handed people are supposed to be good at ball games. There is a higher proportion of top-class sportsmen and women who are left-handers than we would expect from their numbers in the general population. World tennis champions Martina Navratilova, John McEnroe and Rod Laver are all left-handers. Artists, architects and computer experts have a larger-than-expected number of 'lefters' amongst their ranks. One of the world's greatest artistic genuises, Leonardo da Vinci, was left-handed. Though he lived nearly 400 years ago we can tell he was left-handed from his brush strokes, drawings and designs. Strangely enough, people who have problems with speaking and putting words together are often left-handed too.

In everyday life, we are a bit biased against left-handers. Many designs make life difficult − can-openers and scissors, for example. Writing, also, favours right-handers. Try writing this sentence with one hand and then the other. As you write with your right hand you see the words you've just written. When you write with your left hand, notice you cover up the words as you write them. This is important when you learn to write because left-handers cannot see their work until they have written nearly a whole line. Of course, the opposite would happen with Arabic and Hebrew where the writing goes from right to left.

Things to do

1 What are you – left or right-handed? Of course you know already, but try these questions and experiments to find out how you and your friends use your right and left hands. The results may surprise you.

With what hand do you

a write _____

b scratch _____

c comb your hair _____

d pour a drink _____

e hold a spoon _____

f switch on a light _____

g open a door _____

h catch a ball _____

i throw a ball _____

j use a bat _____

Which foot do you use to

k kick a ball   _____

l put forward first when
starting
from the still position   _____

m test the hot water in your
bath?   _____

Which eye do you

n wink with?   _____

If your answers to all these questions are either
Right or Left then you are definitely a one-sided
brain.

If your answers to a, c, d, e, h, i, j and k are all
the same, then you are also one-sided. These actions
use fine control movements. The other actions you
could perform properly with either hand.

If your answers are a complete mix of all these
actions or you can perform most activities with
either hand then you're an all-rounder or ambidextrous. Ambidextrous people are a pretty unusual
lot.

2 Here's an *investigation* you can do on your
friends. Place an object like a pen or a cup on a
table. Find out if your friend is left or right-handed.
If he is left-handed ask him to come to the table
and stand so the object is on his right side. Ask
your right-handed friends to stand with the object
on their left. Then ask them to pick it up. You
should find that the real righters use their right

hand even though it means stretching across to it and the lefters do the same with their left hand. Do this as casually as possible so your friends don't realize what you're trying to do.

Is there a real difference between left- and right-handers besides the side of their body they use most? Are left-handers generally better at games than right-handers? To do this you will need to ask quite a lot of people. If you ask a lot of people you'll get a better answer to your question. Remember, left-handers are fairly difficult to come by – there's only one for every ten people – so get an answer when you meet one. Ask each person if they are good at ball games like soccer, tennis or netball; they don't have to be good at all the games. Ask 20 left-handers and 40 right-handers.

If someone says they are 'average' or 'reasonable', then leave them out. You want people who are either good or poor at ball games.

Write down your answers below:

Names of left-handers   Are they good at ball games?
Yes or No

_____   _____

_____   _____

_____   _____

Names of right-handers   Are they good at ball games?

_____   _____

_____   _____

_____   _____

Out of 20 left-handers I asked __ were good at ball games.

Out of 40 right-handers I asked __ were good at ball games.

Conclusion

It seems that _____ handers are better at ball games than _____ handers.

Are there any other investigations you could carry out? Try and suggest explanations for your results. You can have a lot of fun finding out about the ways we all differ from each other.

One in every ten people is left-handed. Is this ratio true of the people you know? Is it true that left-handers are, on the whole, better at art?

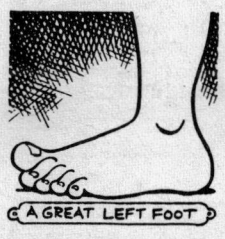

A GREAT LEFT FOOT

Why do we interlock our hands?

We don't usually think about why we interlock our hands. It's an action we perform naturally. If we did think about every movement we made then we wouldn't do very much at all.

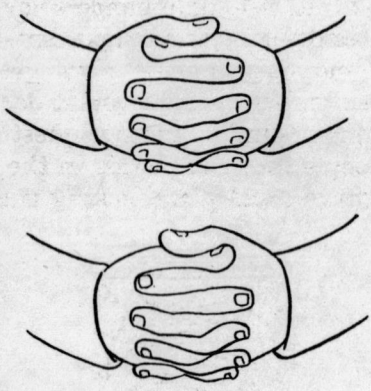

Try it yourself. *(See diagram).* Does your right or left thumb rest on top? Repeat this action so the other thumb rests on top. It doesn't feel quite right, does it? We interlock our hands in one or two ways, and the other way always feels strange. Ask your friends to do this little experiment.

Things to do

Can you suggest a reason for this difference? Do left-handers differ from right-handers in the way they interlock their hands?

1 Ask 20 left-handers and 40 right-handers to perform this action and note down how they differ.

How can you tell if your results mean anything? Suppose the majority of left-handers have one thumb on top and the majority of right-handers have another. You could take another sample and the results might be different. If more than 13 out of your 20 left-handers have one thumb on top, and more than 26 out of 40 right-handers have another, then your results point to an important difference. Try asking more people to see if you get the same kind of results. If your experiment doesn't point to a difference, think of another question to find out why people interlock hands in the way they do. You'll have great fun checking it all out.

Why are we right- or left-eyed?

Are you right- or left-eyed? This question is not as silly as it sounds because you may well use one eye more than the other in the same way that one hand or foot dominates over the other. Here's something to prove it.

Hold a pen or pencil at arm's length. With both eyes open line it up with a distant object. The pencil will look transparent. Now, close first one eye then the other. With one eye the pen will seem to jump from its line with the distant object. This is your weaker eye. It means that the other eye was used more in the lining up.

Things to do

Do right-handed people use their right eye more than their left eye? To find out the answer to this question, you'll have to ask them. Use the table below and ask your friends and school chums to do the little experiment I've just described.

Names of right-handers	What eye do they use more?
_____	_____
_____	_____
_____	_____

Names of left-handers	What eye do they use more?
_____	_____
_____	_____
_____	_____